Whole Heart for Boys

Feeling Good About Yourself

Written by

Amy L. Stark, Ph.D.

Illustrated by

Marvin Alonso

Whole Heart for Boys
Feeling Good About Yourself

This is a work of fiction. Names, characters, places and incidents either are the product of the author's imagination or are used fictitiously, and any resemblanc to any actual persons, living or dead, events, or locales i entirely coincidental.

ISBN 978-1986699150

DEDICATION

I dedicate this book to my mother, Irene.
The woman who always loved me and
cared if I loved myself.

I also dedicate this book in memory of
Mitchell.
Always in our hearts.

CONTENTS

ACKNOWLEDGMENTS

I want to thank all the children and teens I have worked with over the years. Through them, I have learned so much about where self-esteem issues start and the importance of addressing them early on. They have also taught me that self esteem is a journey not a destination. I also wish to thank my editor, Lisa Houser, for her guidance and assistance.

1

DESERVING OF LOVE

"Give it your whole heart." That's what people say to encourage you to do your best. But what if your whole heart isn't whole? What if it has holes in it instead? In fact, what if there are holes where your feelings about you live? How can you give your "whole heart" then?

You were born and you were perfectly loveable. Not because you had all your fingers and toes, or your mother's eyes and your father's chin—but because you truly were a perfect, unique, human being. You didn't even have to DO anything to deserve love.

2

A HEART HOLE

When you went home from the hospital, adults said things to you.

When other adults make mistakes, you think

And a tiny hole in the part of your heart that cares about you appeared.

3

THE HOLE GROWS

Then school starts.

This is what you may hear on the playground. Other kids bully, tease, push or shove.

"It's ok," you would think.

But it wasn't ok.

And the tiny hole in the part of your heart that cares about you grows.

4

SCHOOL & SPORTS

Teachers aren't all the same. Some teachers are supportive and build you up. They praise your efforts and applaud your improvements. Then the hole stays the same for a while—sometimes it even fills in a bit.

Sometimes teachers or grown-ups at the school have bad days, too. They might use a grouchy voice that hurts your feelings. When they tell you what you did wrong, you feel bad, like you can't ever seem to get anything right. And so the hole in the part of your heart that cares about you grows.

Some coaches are positive and they teach you to not give up but to practice. They notice when you try and when you improve. And the hole fills in a bit.

Other coaches scold you when you miss a shot or are not playing your best. They get angry at you and make you feel like you aren't good enough. And so the hole in the part of your heart that cares about you grows.

5

KINDNESS

All around your friends have holes growing. Life's ups and downs affect everyone.

Some become very quiet.

Some try not to make any mistakes.

Some are loud and annoying to gain negative attention instead of no attention at all.

What will you do? You must learn to fill the hole in the part of your heart that cares about you.

No matter what anyone tells you, you deserve love—just like on the day you were born.

And even if someone tells you, 'you are a loser' or laughs at you, don't believe them.

You can find friends who include you and want to hang out with you.

6

THE AMAZING YOU

When you hit a bump in the road—maybe you don't make the team, or your math grade isn't quite what you hoped it would be—remember that it's not the end of the road. Just a bump. There's plenty of road ahead to travel. You can practice, practice, practice for the team and study, study, study your math. You'll soon come to another opportunity to show what you can do. With your hard work, next time you'll shine.

No matter what, you're still loveable. Don't forget to tell yourself how loveable you are. The part of your heart that cares about you likes to hear it.

And since you are in charge of your happily ever after, you will live happily ever after from now on. Oh, but instead of this being the end, this is just the beginning—the beginning of a whole new you.

7

DISCUSSION QUESTIONS

. When you are in a group of friends, how often do you check o make sure you have not left someone out? Why is that mportant?

We have all been left out at one time or another. It does not feel ery good.

Think how nice it would have felt to you if someone would have sked you to join in and be included.

Can you think of a nice way to do that and actually try that at chool?

2. If your friends make fun of someone, how can you discuss how it must feel with them? Is there a way you could reach out to the person they are picking on?

What if you said to your friends that "if someone spoke that way to them it would really hurt their feelings."

Can you talk about something else? Can you go and make sure the person they were picking on is not hurt and tell them you are sorry that happened to them?

. If a teacher or someone at the school is mean or yells at you,
who could you tell? If they do it to someone else, what should
you do?

You should always try to talk to someone at the school first. Tell
grown-up you trust at the school and try to get their help.

Also tell your mom or dad so they can help you.

f a coach is mean to you at a practice, ask your mom and dad
or help.

4. If someone you thought was a friend picks on other people, should you stop them? What if they start to do it to you?

Tell your friend that it makes you sad when they are mean to the other kids. If they are really a good friend maybe they can tell you why they are doing that.

If your friend does that to you, tell them they are hurting your feelings. If they don't seem to care, look around and spend time with someone else.

Maybe your friend is having a bad day. If your friend keeps doing this to you, perhaps you need a break from each other. Tell your friend you want them to be nice to you and if they can't do that, maybe you should each find other friends to be with.

8

ACTIVITIES

. Research the meaning of your name. Why were you given
hat name...ask your parents. Look up the meaning of your
name.

2. Ask 5 people you know what they find special about you. Record their answers

. Write down what you love most about yourself. Leave
oom so that once a year you can re-enter or edit the top 5
hings. Do this for three years.

Amy L. Stark, Ph.D.

ABOUT THE AUTHOR

Dr. Amy Stark, Ph.D. is a highly respected clinical psychologist in the state of California. She received her doctorate in 1981 from the California School of Professional Psychology in San Diego, and her background in education is in child psychology.

Dr. Stark is best known for her work with children in high-conflict divorce situations. One of the unique techniques she brings into play while working with children is the presence of her therapy dog Gregory.

Over the years, many kids and teenagers have attested to how their therapy sessions with Dr. Stark were enhanced by her previous therapy dogs Jimmy and Rita being present. Now with Gregory as the new therapy dog, children feel the same way about him.

Dr. Stark is the author of a series of illustrated children's books The Fairy Godmother Next Door and The Fairy Godmother Babysits plus the self-esteem books Whole Heart for Girls and Whole Heart for Young Women. All of her books are available on amazon.com

For more information: **www.dramystark.com**

Made in the USA
Middletown, DE
17 May 2021